Advanced Studies

for the

CLARINET

by

Victor
POLATSCHEK

First Clarinetist of the Boston Symphony Orchestra

Ed. 1909

G. SCHIRMER, Inc.

DISTRIBUTED BY

HAL•LEONARD®
CORPORATION
7777 W. BLUEMOUND RD. P.O. BOX 13819 MILWAUKEE, WI 53213

CONTENTS

1

Allegro leggero

After Johann Sebastian Bach

Copyright, 1947, by G. Schirmer, Inc.
International Copyright Secured
Printed in the U.S.A.

2

After Hermann Berens

3

After Nikolai Rimsky-Korsakov,
"Scheherazade"

4

After Charles Meyer

10

5

After Dmitri Shostakovich,
Symphony No. 1

6

After Johann Sebastian Bach,
French Suite in C Minor

7

After Stephen Heller

8

After Darius Milhaud,
"Scaramouche"

Vivace

9

Allegro vivace

Victor Polatschek

10

Victor Polatschek

11

After Wolfgang Amadeus Mozart,
Serenade in Bb, K. 361

Allegro moderato

12

After Bedřich Smetana,
String Quartet in E Minor
"Aus meinem Leben"

Allegro moderato

D.C. al Fine

13

After Ludwig van Beethoven

Andante mosso

14

After Richard Strauss,
"Ariadne auf Naxos"*

Tranquillo

* By permission of the copyright owners, Boosey and Hawkes, Inc.

15

After Richard Wagner,
"Die Götterdämmerung"

Allegro moderato

mf

16

Victor Polatschek

17

After William Schuman,
Symphony No. 3

18

After Joseph Sellner

Allegro moderato

19

After Samuel Barber,
Second Essay for Orchestra

Allegro energico ♩.= 144

20

Victor Polatschek

21

After Sergei Prokofieff,
"Overture on Hebrew Themes"

22

Victor Polatschek

Molto vivace

23

After Johann Sebastian Bach

24

After Gustav Mahler,
Symphony No. 4

Allegro moderato

25

After Otto Nicolai,
"Die lustigen Weiber von Windsor"

Allegro moderato

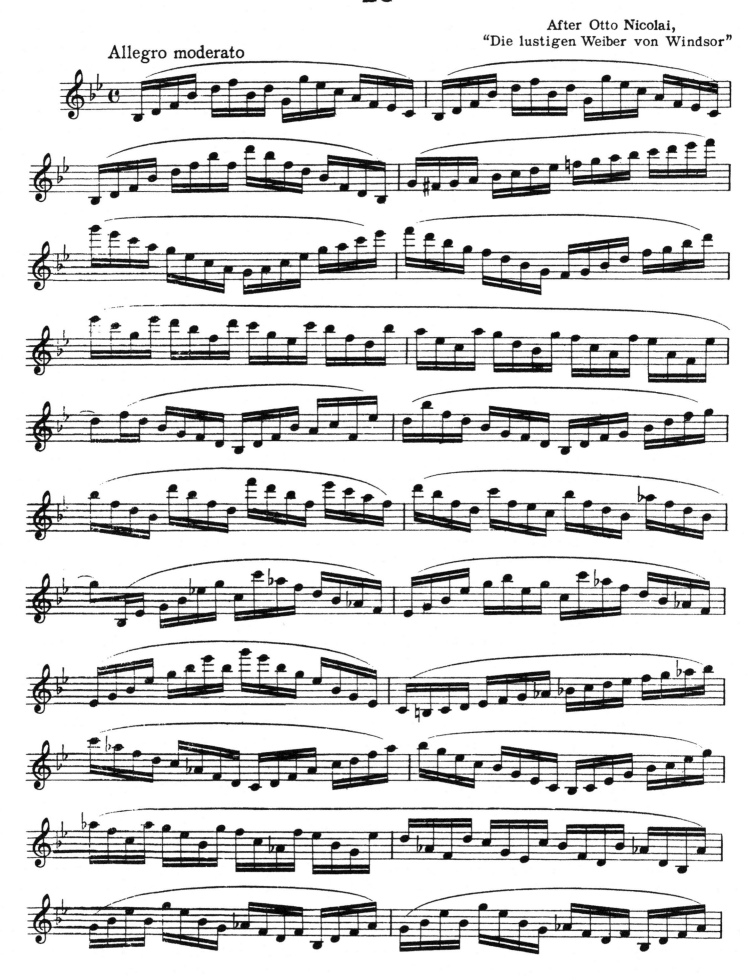

26

After Maurice Ravel,
"Le Tombeau de Couperin"

Molto vivace

27

After Arnold Schoenberg,
"Pierrot Lunaire"*

28

Victor Polatschek

Allegro moderato

ISBN 978-1-4234-4128-1

0-73999-28230-6

51099

G. SCHIRMER, Inc.

DISTRIBUTED BY

HAL•LEONARD®

HL50328230